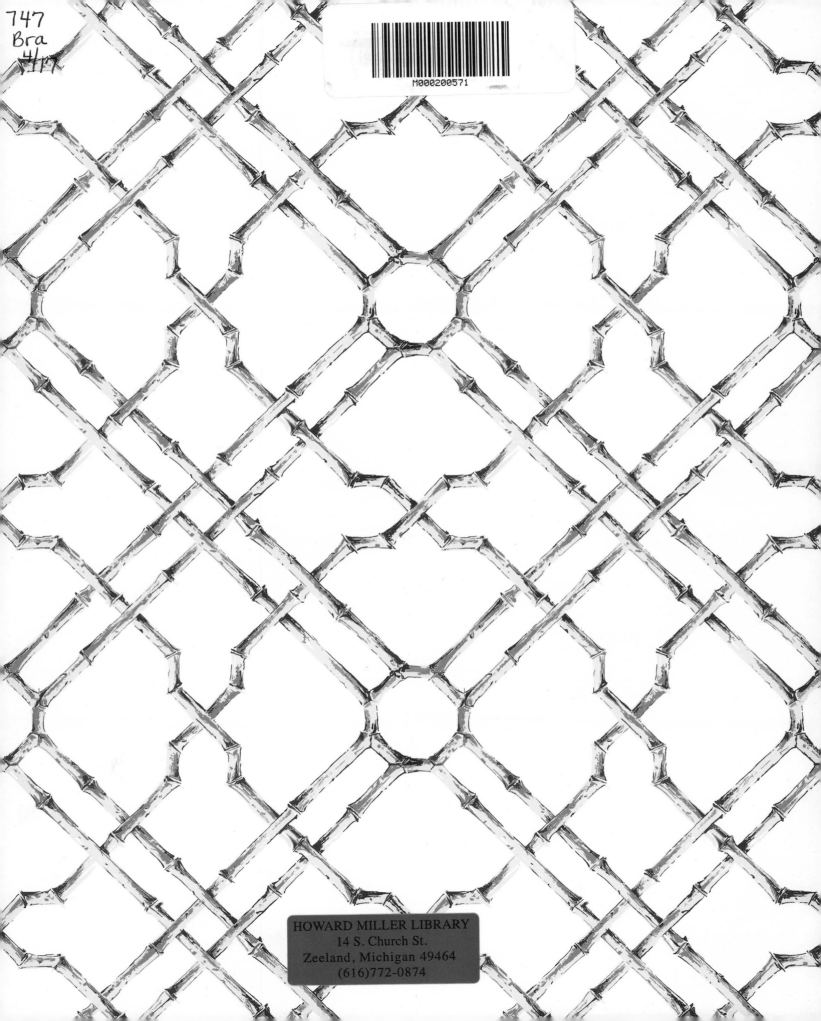

747
Bra
4/17

M000200571

HOWARD MILLER LIBRARY
14 S. Church St.
Zeeland, Michigan 49464
(616)772-0874

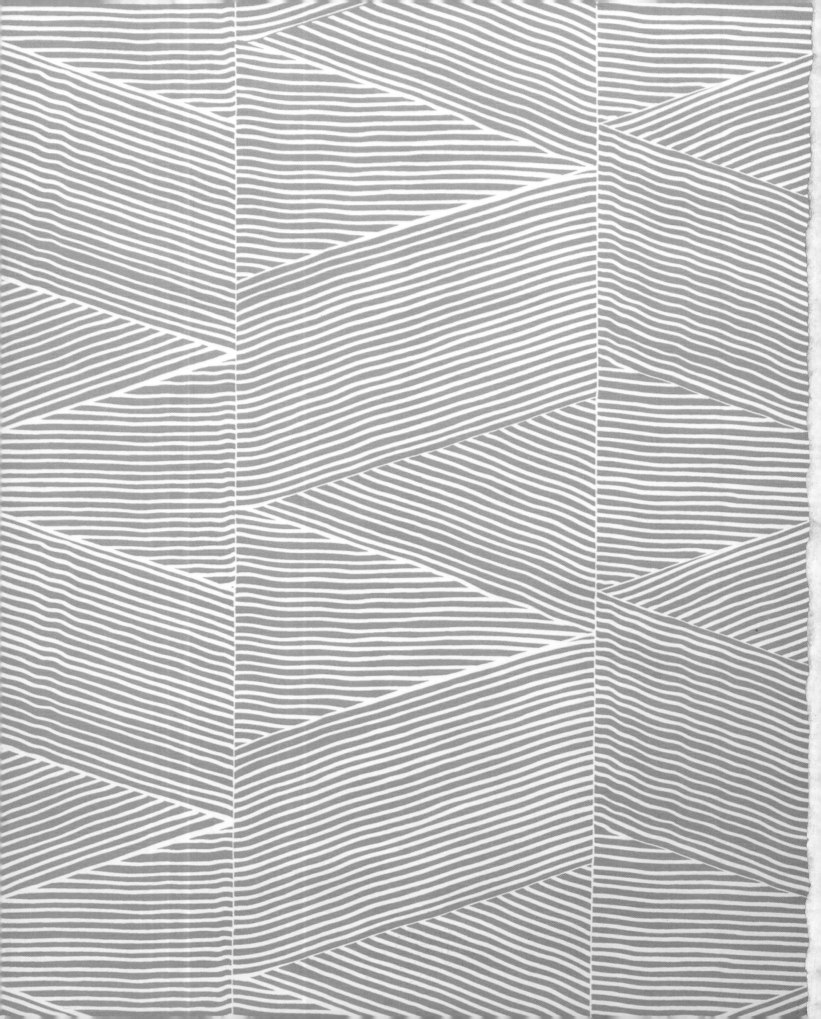

THE DECORATED HOME

Living with Style and Joy

Meg Braff

With Brooke Showell Kasir

FOREWORD BY CHARLOTTE MOSS
Photography by J. Savage Gibson

RIZZOLI
NEW YORK

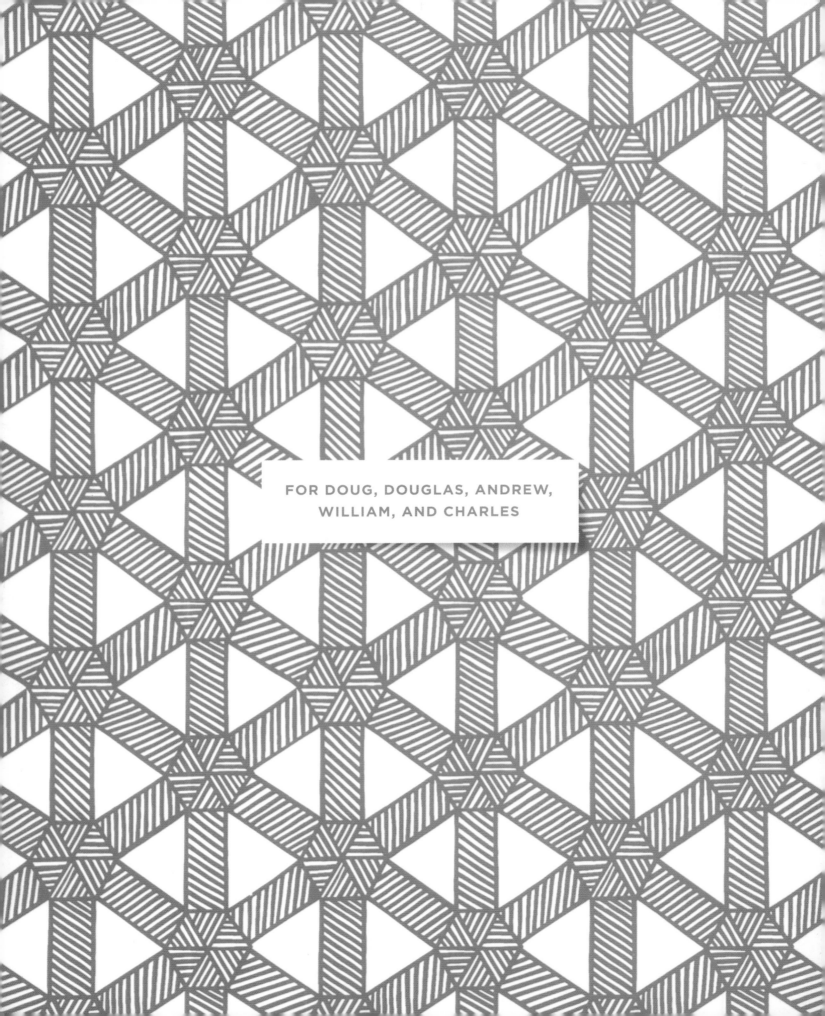

FOR DOUG, DOUGLAS, ANDREW,
WILLIAM, AND CHARLES

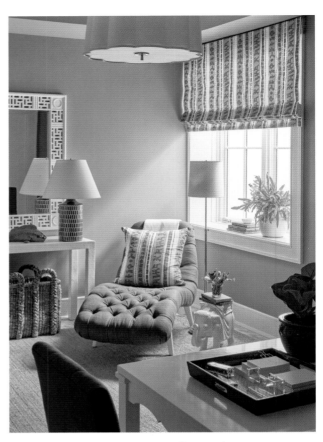

Foreword
By Charlotte Moss

PERHAPS THE MOST IMPORTANT QUALITY IN DESIGN IS THE ABILITY TO FOLLOW ONE'S INSTINCTS. Meg Braff followed hers, first by starting her now well-established firm twenty years ago, then opening a design store in Locust Valley, next acquiring the Philip Graf wallpaper archives and making them her own, and finally writing this, her first book.

MEG IS ONE OF THOSE PEOPLE WHO IMMEDIATELY ADDS A SENSE OF GAIETY TO A ROOM. Her spaces are filled with bold patterns, bright happy colors, and a sense of celebration. There is uniqueness to her process that draws from her ebullient personality.

THIS ENTHUSIASM IS CONTAGIOUS AND EVIDENCES ITSELF IN HER JOYOUS COLOR SCHEMES AND FRESH, CLEAN SPIN ON CLASSIC DESIGN THAT RESULTS IN HOMES THAT ARE WELL-LIVED IN AND THOROUGHLY ENJOYED. Meg's optimism, confidence, and commitment to her own aesthetic are her greatest strengths.

CREATING BEAUTIFUL ROOMS FOR MEG IS ABOUT FINDING THE UNIQUE AND THE UNPREDICTABLE AND HER ATTITUDE TOWARD THE HUNT ENERGIZES HER CLIENTS AS MUCH AS THEIR INTERIORS. Like the cocktail party in *Breakfast at Tiffany's*, with its pop-pop fizz-fizz Henry Mancini score, Meg's effervescence is evidenced in her rooms, and in this book. Beautifully photographed and crisply written with the sound advice of a pro, *The Decorated Home: Living with Style and Joy* will excite you, inspire you, and guide you in your journey to a beautiful, happy home.

Happiness at Home

HAPPINESS FOR ME IS DEFINED BY MY HUSBAND AND BOYS, AND THE SPIRIT OF HOME THAT WE CREATE WHENEVER WE ARE TOGETHER. Nothing brings me more delight than creating a beautiful space my family can enjoy. Similarly, in all of my projects, my top priority is to create a warm and welcoming environment that reflects and uplifts my client's lifestyle. It doesn't matter how big or small, formal or informal, your home is. The most beautiful decoration comes from the thoughtful approach of unearthing unpredictable and serendipitous finds that make a space feel unique and special. Every detail should elicit joy.

THE TREASURE-HUNT MIND-SET HAS ALWAYS BEEN A PART OF ME, AND I CULTIVATED IT EARLY ON. When I was growing up in Tupelo, Mississippi, my mother lovingly incorporated many pretty antiques that once belonged to my grandparents throughout our home. She also really enjoys entertaining, and, like me, she collects interesting porcelain and table settings. The two of us are constantly scouring places for just the right things to mix in. For me, the ultimate design high comes from finding one-of-a-kind (and, more often than you might think, inexpensive) items at auctions and estate sales and refurbishing them with custom paint or upholstery to make them feel personal to their new space. Over the years, these types of pieces have become part of my design signature.

YOU COULD SAY THAT MY FIRST DECORATING PROJECT WAS THE APARTMENT MY ROOMMATE, BETH, AND I SHARED DURING OUR SENIOR YEAR AT VANDERBILT UNIVERSITY. The two of us amassed a pile of odds and ends from friends and family, and we had a ton of fun decorating and reconfiguring our space to make those pieces our own. I loved my first foray into decorating, and after graduation, it propelled me to move to New York and attend Parsons School of Design.

MY PROFESSORS AT PARSONS INSTILLED IN ME THE IMPORTANCE OF STUDYING THE WORK OF DESIGNERS AND ARCHITECTS I ADMIRED, AN ESSENTIAL FACET OF DESIGN THAT I ALWAYS SHARE WITH THE YOUNG PEOPLE WORKING IN MY OFFICE. Having a design mentor is as valuable as formal training, and he or she can provide lessons that cannot be gleaned from a classroom. I am blessed to have the friendship of celebrated designer Charlotte Moss, who wrote the

foreword to this book. Charlotte was a role model for me from the beginning of my career, and she remains a decorating inspiration to this day. When I was just starting out in New York, I frequented Charlotte's glorious decorating shop on Lexington Avenue. It is a testament to her uncanny eye and good taste that the purchases I made from her curated store are still with me some twenty-five years later.

FROM THE PAST, I'VE ALWAYS FELT A KINSHIP WITH THE DESIGNER FRANCES ELKINS, WHO WAS QUITE PROLIFIC IN THE 1930S AND '40S AND KNOWN FOR HER FEMININE YET STREAMLINED AESTHETIC. Like Elkins, I embrace color, chinoiserie, and furnishings that encompass modern and traditional. Photos of her work continue to inspire me, whether it's how she played with scale or the tiny details on a tailored slipcover.

WHILE WORKING UNDER THE TUTELAGE OF ESTABLISHED DESIGNERS IN NEW YORK CITY, I BEGAN TO SPREAD MY WINGS AND TAKE ON A FEW PROJECTS OF MY OWN. Sometimes when you are first starting out, the only people eager to hire you are your relatives, and redecorating for my family in Mississippi and my mother-in-law in New York City allowed me to experiment with how to incorporate a gracious sense of Southern tradition into vibrant, modern homes. I realized that this inviting philosophy translates well anywhere, and my designs today remain under the gentle influence of the South, no matter where my work takes me.

IN 1994, I OFFICIALLY OPENED MY OWN FIRM, MEG BRAFF DESIGNS, AND OVER THE YEARS I HAVE TAKEN ON PROJECTS IN SOME RATHER DREAMY LOCATIONS: THE HAMPTONS, PALM BEACH, NEWPORT, JAMAICA, SEA ISLAND. I strive to personalize each project so that it reflects not only the home's location and architecture, but also the personality of clients. Do they frequently entertain for twelve, or do they prefer curling up as a family in front of the fire? Is it all about an outdoor deck for sundowners with the neighbors, or do the kids pile into the family room for movie night?

THE YEAR 2011 BROUGHT TWO EXCITING CHANGES. First, I acquired the archives of midcentury wallpaper company Philip Graf and started out on my mission to modernize his gorgeous patterns. Reimagining and recoloring these wallpapers is a wonderful creative process, and every time I dive in, it is like a gift. I also opened a store,

Meg Braff Antiques & Decoration, in Locust Valley, New York. As a designer, having a store is such a luxury. I'm able to buy the things I love and hope they find a great home—and until then, I get to enjoy them. The store is our think tank where we're constantly experimenting with looks, anticipating what works, and generating ideas. My office is also situated within the shop, so I can meet customers who stop by to share their design dilemmas and to visit with our staff.

AS OF WRITING THIS BOOK, WE ARE BUILDING A NEW HOME TO REPLACE THE ONE DOUG AND OUR FOUR BOYS HAVE LIVED IN FOR THE PAST SEVENTEEN YEARS. As much as I love our old home, building a new one has been an exciting experience: Decorating should be one of your happiest times, and every project begins with so much optimism about the creative challenge ahead. Even that first trip to the tile store is filled with enthusiasm. But it can also be an overwhelming process; especially as a designer, there are so many wonderful options that it can be hard to commit. I'm trying to really go for it and push my choices, because that's what I always encourage my clients to do. Like them, I'm looking forward to installation, which is always the most joyful day because everything finally comes together.

GREAT DECORATING DOESN'T HAPPEN IN A DAY BUT IS EVER EVOLVING. Like playing the piano, the more you practice, the better you'll get at hitting the right notes. Throughout these pages, I will walk you through how to incorporate bold color without hesitation, mix and match intriguing patterns and textures that sing together, and layer each room with finishing touches that feel purposeful and full of personality. Once you've turned on your decorator brain, you might notice it starts to pull you toward consistent ideas. Personally, I return to the crisp bedding, chinoiserie, bamboo and rattan, pagoda shapes, lacquered pieces, Lucite, and vintage brass that make up my recipe for a pretty and welcoming room.

MOST IMPORTANTLY, YOUR HOME SHOULD REFLECT YOU. A thoughtfully detailed house feels fresh and clean and engages all of your senses, as if you have the windows open and are letting life in. Even more than the perfect pagoda lantern, we all respond to the smell of a fire in the fireplace, the fragrance of a favorite candle, the scent of fresh laundry, or a waft of something delicious baking in the oven. If it's more important to have a yoga mat than a sofa in your living room, I say go for it. In the end, when you start your day amid the furnishings and accessories that bring you joy, you walk out the door a happier person. In this book, I hope to inspire you to do just that.

In Pursuit of Color

IN DECORATION, COLOR IS A POWERFUL TOOL. It evokes strong feelings and memories. It's usually the first thing you notice in a room, and it can be a point of differentiation between spaces. I'm inherently drawn to a cheerful palate. Sunny colors like turquoise-blue and citrus-yellow play a starring role in my rooms.

WHEN I WAS A TEENAGER IN MISSISSIPPI AND READY FOR A LITTLE REFRESH, I REDECORATED MY BEDROOM WITH A HAPPY AND BRIGHT APPLE GREEN PAINT COLOR. At the time, our design resources were somewhat limited, but it was a very big deal to me that I was permitted to help my mother select colorful bedding from the Ralph Lauren store, the prettiest Schumacher chintz fabric for the curtains with greens and blues and a touch of Chinese coral, and a green trellis carpet. My family inherited a beautiful old bed from my grandmother, and it had always felt quite grand to be the guardian of such a precious antique. But suddenly, the color in the room was fresh, new, and all mine. I'm just as invigorated today by colors that feel completely personalized—the peppy turquoise carpet in my twins' room that matches their boundless energy, or the subtle pale lavender we chose for a young girl's bedroom that's sweet yet sophisticated enough to grow with her.

COLOR MAKES ME HAPPY. Intense hues lift my spirits and calm my nerves. While we all have our aesthetic comfort zone, don't be afraid to use color to make an impact in your home. A saturated aubergine adds drama and warmth to a dining room in the evening. An energetic orange and white tile might be just right for mornings in the kitchen. Spend some time thinking about what colors make you feel good.

AND JUST AS YOUR PALETTE SHOULD SUIT YOUR PERSONALITY, IT SHOULD ALSO SUIT YOUR LOCALE. Colors sing together and hit different notes depending on where you are. In Locust Valley, New York, classic choices—warm reds, buttoned-up blues, and rich ocher yellows—feel right among the charming old world architecture. On the other hand, in a modern Palm Beach pied-à-terre, tropical pinks, oranges, and crisp whites are vivid enough to stand up to the gorgeous Florida sunlight.

IN THE MOST THOUGHTFULLY DESIGNED HOMES, EACH ROOM SHOULD FEEL CONNECTED TO THE NEXT. Think of how color will flow and transition throughout the space. Having continuity prevents a house from feeling too much like a rainbow, with every corner a different hue. Some areas are conducive to full-on color, while others call for a more understated moment to strike the right balance. Spreading around color and contrast allows the eye to enjoy bold punctuation on the walls in one room, then on the floor in the next, and maybe even on the ceiling or inside of a closet in another. Suddenly, the color story makes sense.

THE MOST INTRIGUING PAINT COLORS ARE THOSE THAT ARE JUST OFFBEAT ENOUGH TO CATCH YOUR EYE. Green is still a color I use almost as a neutral thanks to its many nuances; like the flowers in a garden, all other colors simply look good against it. The secret is that the variations need not match exactly. There's nothing prettier than mixing an edgy chartreuse with a more traditional grassy color to add a little zip. Such an elusive pairing has great impact because it's slightly unexpected.

HOWEVER, IF I HAD TO ALIGN WITH ONE COLOR, IT WOULD BE BLUE. I am captivated by many shades of blue, from the soothing, expressive Prussian blues in Henri Matisse paintings to the intriguing, muted tones of the French artist Roger Mühl. Combining similar blues and greens in a room can be overwhelmingly elegant and beautiful. Billy Baldwin, one of the most revered designers of the twentieth century, did this to great effect in his iconic blue salon at La Fiorentina, on the French Riviera in the 1970s. Blue evokes the ocean and air; similar to green, it takes on a neutral quality because it works so well with other colors. To create a sense of fluidity, I love to repeat a touch of blue from room to room, such as a thread in a carpet, the hue of a wall, or the edging on a lampshade.

IF YOU HAVE A TENDENCY TO DECORATE WITH A LOT OF WHITE, GRAY, AND BEIGE, TRY TO INCORPORATE COLOR SPARINGLY AT FIRST. Adding a rich throw pillow, a pair of custom glazed lamps, or a piece of art is less intimidating than splashing an entire wall in magenta. Rooms can typically take a lot more color than you think. I often feel like there is space for another layer, or a burst of Chinese red, teal, or daffodil. Remember, color itself is timeless—it only feels trendy or dated based on how it's used.

Evoking the ocean and air, timeless blue can take on an inviting neutral quality in any room. Here, repetition of the hue on walls, window shades, and chairs beautifies a home office in Southampton, New York.

PREVIOUS SPREAD: A pair of large, low-slung upholstered 1970s sofas make an impact with a concentrated splash of ocean blue and provide a bit of a throwback and nods to the midcentury vibe of a 1960s Sea Island, Georgia, home. RIGHT: Color lends energy to durable fabrics, and the various blues in the room—aqua fabric shades, denim-colored sofas, and navy raffia walls—perk up the nearly bulletproof furnishings chosen for this family with young children. A rustic chandelier and textured natural-fiber rug take the edge off the concentration of blue, and a chartreuse table lamp adds a nice contrast.

ABOVE: Accessories made from natural materials, and an eclectic mirror framed in wood with inlaid ivory, neutralize the saturated color of a striking chartreuse wall. OPPOSITE: Every room should feel fresh and modern, but also like it has collected memories over time. In a brand-new sitting room, blue and green are a restful combination that always works for entertaining, napping, or reading by the fire. A traditional English-arm sofa, an old-fashioned marble-topped coffee table purchased at an estate sale, and small colorful porcelain objects add age and depth.

RIGHT: Color choices should suit your locale. A Palm Beach, Florida, sitting room that faces the water mirrors the ocean with a strong turquoise palette. The vivid hue on a large daybed and armchairs helps to distract the eye from a rarely used door. FOLLOWING SPREAD: Colors need not always be jolting, and neutral hues like buttery yellow, misty blue, and soft green offer great dimension. Painted sconces, a large glass coffee table, and a tall plant add height and scale.

HOWARD MILLER LIBRARY
ZEELAND, MI 49464

RIGHT: Rooms can typically take a lot more color than one might think. Orange is a hot choice that radiates on lamps, armchairs, and Roman shades in a Quadrille fabric. Against textured grass-cloth walls in warm and inviting daffodil yellow, the bright color feels right for a sunny location.

FOLLOWING SPREAD: Color can be a little more daring in a summer home. Bright blue and crisp white keep a pool house fresh and casual. It's all about the pretty yet sturdy fabric on comfortable seating and a subtle wool geometric rug that withstands wet feet.

Like flowers in a verdant garden, many colors look pleasing against a green base. Painting a sitting room's trim nearly the same chartreuse color as the grass-cloth walls draws the eye outward to the glorious view. Grass cloth's organic texture warms up a room and often creates more depth than painting, glazing, or even lacquering. Throw pillows are in Meg Braff Designs Beverly Hills fabric.

ABOVE AND OPPOSITE: Offbeat shades are especially interesting in a designer showhouse.
Chartreuse walls in a bedroom take on a glamorous feel with all the right details: a Chinese black-
lacquered nightstand, a vividly framed round mirror, a fun fur throw, a vintage chair covered
in a tiger silk velvet and custom headboard in Meg Braff Designs Forbidden City fabric.

Neutral furnishings with simple lines let a pairing of intense Kelly green and crisp white take the forefront in an East Hampton, New York, master bedroom.

RIGHT: Apricot is cheerful and welcoming, yet it lends the right degree of formality and elegance. The shape of a comfortable upholstery armchair keeps it from feeling too precious. Buy things you love: One well-chosen painting can inspire and pull together an entire room's palette. FOLLOWING SPREAD: Sunny chevron curtains and thin bamboo floor lamps add a youthful feel while not obstructing views of Long Island Sound. Natural light pouring through the windows is the best way to illuminate a room's palette.

Yellow, Chinese red, and blue are a classic design trifecta for a traditional home. Asian art is a great tool in decorating when you're looking for something interesting and beautiful on a large scale. Its vast range mixes well with pieces and palettes from other periods.

ABOVE AND OPPOSITE: Consider how color flows and transitions throughout the home, so that each room feels connected to the next. A signature move: painting out the trim to make a city pied-à-terre feel more seamless. In a library, black trim that matches black grass-cloth walls makes the ceiling appear higher, more open, and less choppy.

ABOVE AND OPPOSITE: Bursts of color and contrast create a sense of bold punctuation from room to room. A touch of the exotic always makes an impact. Mixing multihued patterns of different scales, such as a fun tiger carpet and a Chinese-inspired fabric on the curtains on bamboo rods, adds lightness to a dark space.

I Have a Thing for Pattern

COCO CHANEL ONCE ADVISED, "BEFORE YOU LEAVE THE HOUSE, LOOK IN THE MIRROR AND TAKE ONE THING OFF." You should follow the same advice when decorating with pattern. Like fashion, pattern benefits from a good edit.

Take the sunroom of my home in Locust Valley. Its trellis carpet and yellow-checked curtains pop against chartreuse glazed walls and have withstood any redecorating whims I may have had—seventeen years later, the room is just as lovely. It's a success because the scale is spot-on, the color is balanced, and just the right amount of pattern delightfully mixes together. Think layered but restrained—the leopard stool I was itching to use threw the optics off balance in this space, but later it felt just right in a client's study.

PATTERN IS EVOCATIVE; IT CAN TRANSPORT YOU TO SOMEPLACE WARM AND WONDERFUL, OR SOPHISTICATED AND ZEN. Try to create interiors with details that call to their surroundings—chic vintage dining chairs with antique tole palm trees in Florida, sofas swathed in island fauna in a Jamaica living room, or a genteel trellis wallpaper in an Upper East Side apartment that reminds me of white-gloved ladies at the Colony Club. Just as you consider the transition of color from room to room, think about a balance of pattern that gradually reveals itself throughout your home.

Like color, a room can typically withstand a little more pattern than one may think. I always encourage pushing the proverbial envelope a bit—the fanciful accent of a zebra rug against a more studious Chippendale chair feels refreshing.

ON THE OTHER HAND, IT'S RATHER HEADACHE-INDUCING TO ENTER A ROOM SO OVERWHELMED BY PATTERN THAT YOU DON'T KNOW WHERE TO LOOK FIRST. Luckily, such an overdose is easily reversible. A well-meaning client once added a patterned carpet to her living room that was just one thing too many—its artful swirls, while pretty on their own, added too much color and density and didn't leave any breathing room. We had to pull back a notch and replace it with a simpler sisal rug, which I think of as the great neutralizer. This quick change balanced the space and took the edge off all of the layers.

WHILE THERE IS NO EXACT FORMULA, LAYERS OF PATTERN WORK BEST WHEN YOU MIX SCALES. A small ikat on a lampshade next to a chair covered in a larger pattern creates a mix that's visually intriguing. Aim for interest at different heights in the room; don't concentrate all the pattern at eye level or on the floor.

WHEN CHOOSING PATTERNS, LOOK TO YOUR HOME'S SURROUNDINGS AND HERITAGE FOR INSPIRATION. Today, my family spends much of our time in Newport, Rhode Island, which has a long history of Chinese influence—just study one of the fanciful chic bedrooms in Doris Duke's Rough Point estate. I am smitten with all things Asian—pagoda shapes, bamboo shoots, Chinese peonies, and Chinese export porcelain, to name a few. Chinoiserie's glamour, fun, and whimsy never go out of style. In my own house, I've juxtaposed those exotic scenes with cheerful, unpretentious East Coast checks, which tone down fussier, more formal patterns.

I'M ALSO IN LOVE WITH MIDCENTURY PATTERNS, AND FOR YEARS I'VE BEEN REVIVING DESIGNS FROM THE ARCHIVES OF THE PHILIP GRAF WALLPAPER COMPANY. The gorgeous classic prints are rich with old-Hollywood style—I have just updated the colors for today's sensibilities. Patterned wallpaper is one of the most useful tools designers have in their bag of tricks. There are endless possibilities in how to use it, especially in a newer house or a room without carpeting. It's an extra decorative layer that can add warmth and detail to a space lacking remarkable architecture, transform a cavernous room into an intimate retreat, or even out awkward angles and make a quirky space feel cohesive. The trick is to think outside the box with wallpaper—try using it in bookshelves, closets, or even on the ceiling.

AND MOST OF ALL, NEVER LET YOUR PATTERN CHOICES GET TOO SERIOUS. Use your imagination and have fun with it.

Decorating with exotic patterns indulges worldly passions. Chinese-inspired, custom-colored blue-and-green Nanking wallpaper by Meg Braff Designs, framed by peacock blue trim, unifies and transports a small bar space.

PREVIOUS SPREAD: When faced with ordinary millwork, painting out the trim in a satin finish and adding pops of energetic pattern help everything to look a bit more updated. ABOVE: A simple arrangement of rannculus (my favorite flowers) complements the room's colors. OPPOSITE: Wallpaper is an excellent starting place to consider pattern. A Palm Beach apartment centers around the strong scale and color of bamboo and birds—a fitting background for the whimsy of a vintage orange sofa.

PREVIOUS SPREAD, LEFT: Chinese lattice wallpaper makes a big first impression and adds a desired architectural element. The graphic touch gives a burst of energy to a room needing a little character. PREVIOUS SPREAD, RIGHT: The finishing touch of an artful vase adds personality to a sunny workplace. RIGHT: In lieu of art that might compete with patterned furnishings, a rattan mirror lightens a beach house's family room. Natural-fiber rugs are like a classic white T-shirt upon which you can build a decorating wardrobe—swap it out in colder months for a wool version or layer a small patterned rug on top for added coziness and color. FOLLOWING SPREAD, LEFT: Charming accessories in solid colors, whether an antique book, cashmere blanket or lacquered lamp, subdue a riot of pattern. FOLLOWING SPREAD, RIGHT: Bamboo chairs dressed up with ikat cushions add whimsy to a family games table.

HOWARD MILLER LIBRARY
ZEELAND, MI 49464

PREVIOUS SPREAD: Even traditional decorating feels at home with a wealth of pattern. The classically symmetrical layout of a family den—layered with bold gestures, from a Chinese rug to a tiger throw pillow nestled on the velvet sofa—looks to have organically evolved over time and begs one to sit and stay awhile. LEFT AND ABOVE: Blue-striped walls and an antique rug in a library create a comfortable yet tailored feeling to assuage the buttoned-up aesthetic of Newport, Rhode Island.

OPPOSITE AND ABOVE: A beachy, breezy striped rug provides a clue that a TV room is designed as a family hangout. The durable custom cotton sectional and rattan armchairs upholstered in a Chinese dragon fabric are meant to be moved around for watching movies or playing pool.

A saturation of blue and green
patterns creates a bright
and airy space for summer.
A modern zigzag cotton
Indian dhurrie and
leopard-print pillows
add zip to this cheerful room.

ABOVE: Pattern need not be limited to walls and furnishings. The dynamic lines of a custom staircase modernize the 1940s feel of a Regency-style home. OPPOSITE: A printed fabric on a guest bedroom's bed and Roman shades is whimsical but appropriately restful in subdued beige and white. Patterns of different scales add layers of interest, especially when working with understated neutrals.

ABOVE AND OPPOSITE: Mixing eclectic seating purchased at auction—from 1970s Parsons lounge chairs in a geometric taupe fabric to a small Chinese-inspired blue linen ottoman—creates warmth around the hearth. High-backed armchairs in an ikat flank the fireplace and offer extra seating in a tight spot.

OPPOSITE AND ABOVE: A monochromatic pattern on a bedroom's walls envelops it in beautiful, restful blue. The scale of my Meadow Reed wallpaper plays to this master bedroom's generous proportions.

ABOVE: In a traditional home, a careful repetition of subdued pattern maintains a sense of calm.
OPPOSITE: A large-scale Bennison cotton paisley fabric on a thin brass curtain pole adds warmth and scale to this 1930s paneled library. The tomato-red velvet sofa and Indian carpet are luxurious choices to mix in.

A modern geometric fabric on thin brass curtain poles lightens the aesthetic of a rich wood-paneled library. The home's existing upholstered sofas get a fresh look with new throw pillows and a custom dhurrie carpet.

OPPOSITE: A wooden games table, lacquered a pale green and paired with rich cut-velvet armchairs, gives a family library extra purpose, whether it's dinner for two or Scrabble for four. ABOVE: Chairs upholstered in chocolate-brown velvet and Meg Braff Designs Fern wallpaper custom-colored in gray create a neutral effect in a sun-filled loggia. A midcentury brass games table allows the room's natural light to bounce off its glass top, and a bar cart attractively organizes drinks so you are always prepared for company.

In an awkwardly shaped bonus room, an exciting rainforest wallpaper keeps the eye moving and camouflages architectural imperfections. Straw matting on the floor furthers the jungle effect without overpowering it.

ABOVE: A bold parquet floor in an entryway adds interest in a space where a carpet would have been cumbersome. A subtle mélange of tan and cream—from a Greek-key stair runner to palm-tree wallpaper— allows the eye to travel. OPPOSITE: Elements in a bedroom can be simple, but monochromatic does not have to mean flat. Island-influenced custom-colored Meg Braff Designs Nassau wallpaper dramatically envelops without overwhelming. Seashells on the walls and embroidered bed linens are chicly modern.

It's in the Details

EVEN WHEN THE WALLS ARE PAINTED A BEAUTIFUL BLUE, THE FURNITURE IS UPHOLSTERED IN WELL-CHOSEN FABRICS, THE CHANDELIER IS SPARKLING, AND THE CARPETS ARE CUSHY UNDERFOOT, A HOME IS STILL NOT COMPLETE. When I work with a client, I hope to get about eighty-five percent of the way to completion. Leaving a little breathing space at the end allows you to find great treasures down the road and put your own stamp on each room.

GREAT DECORATING DOESN'T HAPPEN IN A DAY, BUT BELIEVE ME, IT WILL COME TOGETHER OVER TIME. Every room needs a little wow factor, and to achieve a space where everything feels impactful and evolved, you always want to be looking. It's similar to Christmas shopping: Instead of running out to buy everything in one fell swoop, throughout the year I am on the hunt for just the right gifts for my friends and family. Once I find them, I keep them in my little hiding place until December rolls around.

CONSIDER WHERE YOU WANT TO DRAW THE EYE. In every room there is some point of inspiration, whether it's a fantastic carpet you found in your travels or a beautiful painting that would be just perfect over the mantel. Make choices that complement your home, and choose focal points wisely. If you love your sofa, add a chic lumbar pillow to draw the eye. If you have a pair of lamps that feel a bit plain, custom lampshades add punch.

THERE'S SOMETHING TO BE SAID FOR BUYING THINGS YOU LOVE FIRST AND INCORPORATING THEM INTO THE HOME LATER. I have the luxury of running a store, so I buy whatever I'm drawn to—an elegant games table or a vintage brass mirror—and am elated when I finally find a place for it, whether it's for my own home or with a client.

A GOOD STARTING POINT IS SHOPPING FOR ANTIQUES AND VINTAGE PIECES. I prefer to own things that have been loved, and to enjoy their rich and unique stories. I adore finding beautiful accessories at auctions or estate sales with a little age and pedigree that will add depth to a room. Pieces like an old suzani can bring pattern and texture when draped over the back of a sofa, just as a vintage rock crystal chandelier can add glamour and sophistication to a dining room. One of my favorite experiences was an estate sale on New York's

Long Island at a house decorated by Mario Buatta. A lot of people with excellent taste, including Cornelia Guest, Harry Hinson, and Albert Hadley, were competing for the same splendid items. In addition to some beautifully-made curtains, lacquered coffee tables, vintage mirrored Hansen standing lamps, and fantastic-looking works of art, I bought the most exquisite pair of black-lacquered chinoiserie screens that I have stored for thirteen years and which are now going straight into my new house. Not only was it thrilling to be bidding against some of the world's most iconic designers, but it is exciting to know the screens I bought more than a decade ago now finally have a home.

JUXTAPOSING THOSE STORY-FILLED ANTIQUES WITH NEWER PIECES—A PRETTY TORTOISESHELL BOX OR A MODERN LACQUER TRAY FOR A SHOT OF COLOR— MAKES A SPACE FEEL IMBUED WITH LAYERS OF INTEREST. It's easier to appreciate beautiful things if they have a point of contrast, and mixing styles and eras is what brings character to a space. Every room wants to feel contemporary, but also like it's been there for some time.

AS YOU COLLECT, THINK ABOUT WHY YOU'RE KEEPING AN OBJECT. We can become attached to possessions for the wrong reason—perhaps you wildly overpaid for something and feel guilty letting it go. I have a wonderful client with a great eye who was passionate about art and had also inherited pieces from her mother-in-law. She wanted to continue looking for paintings that better suited her personality and design aesthetic, so we placed what she had in locations where it did not dictate the design of the room. A less-loved portrait went into the upstairs landing, and a lovely modern oil that she could not quite connect to went into the hallway. The rearranging left six or seven prime spots to showcase pieces she truly loved, and it was a treat to go back five years later to see what she had acquired to give the home her own personal touch.

PRACTICE RESTRAINT: WHAT YOU DON'T BUY IS JUST AS IMPORTANT AS WHAT YOU DO BUY. Avoid the trap of living with things that weigh you down and prevent you from having the house you always wanted. An inherited carpet may be worth a nominal amount, but you might end up spending a small fortune decorating around it. Sell it, donate it to your favorite charity, or put it in a guest room where it has limited exposure. Shoot for the moon and think about the perfect piece—and then go and find exactly that.

PREVIOUS SPREAD: A large gilt wood starburst mirror anchors a large wall in a Locust Valley living room. Ladylike pleats on a classic sofa are mixed with layers of apricot pillows and a few beautiful inherited pieces. OPPOSITE: Whether from a favorite florist or fresh cut from the garden, simple blooms add an element of nature in any season.

PREVIOUS SPREAD:
European antiques and
Asian pieces mix well with
newer finds in this space.
A large mirror reflects the
garden outside, and a
three-paneled leather
screen conveys height and
scale. RIGHT: Even when
you're just getting started
on a decorating a room,
think through to where
you're headed. Color-
drenched pops of yellow
highlight sunny views of
the Intracoastal Waterway
in this Palm Beach home.
Lucite is an unobtrusive
choice for a coffee table
that doesn't obstruct
striped cotton rugs sewn
together. A Lucite étagère
discreetly tucks into a
corner and holds a TV.

HOWARD MILLER LIBRARY
ZEELAND, MI 49464

RIGHT: Whimsical Asian accessories paired with midcentury-modern chairs and gilt finishes pepper a high-rise apartment influenced by interior designer James Mont. A flokati rug softens the harder edges of the masculine green, brown, and gold palette.
FOLLOWING SPREAD: A Florida family room centers around the local sea life. Custom-framed images reference the nearby ocean and provide scale on a large wall. Subtle pops of pattern in throw pillows and the rug add interest to solid upholstery.

ABOVE: A slightly challenging space like an upstairs loft is an opportunity to repurpose favorite furnishings. A vintage Lucite dining table doubles as a desk, a daybed tucked in front of the window is the perfect spot to enjoy the view, and a console gets new life when painted blue. OPPOSITE: Every room needs a little wow factor. A nine-foot-tall vintage brass palm tree is also a standing lamp and gives scale to a room with sixteen-foot ceilings. It's a striking metallic pop alongside a vintage sofa reupholstered in my Nassau fabric and a custom-designed cotton dhurrie that anchor the adjacent seating area.

LEFT AND ABOVE: Beloved books need not be confined to shelves, but make for intriguing conversation pieces when artfully stacked on a coffee table or console. One can never have too many vases or trays—collect them on your travels and rotate them periodically throughout the home to give each room fresh perspective.

ABOVE: Adding a bar to a library invites guests to make themselves at home. RIGHT: A modern bronze coffee table with a custom Saint Laurent marble top anchors the seating area of a paneled library. Even a traditional room can have an element of surprise and exoticism, such as the unexpected flokati fabric on Asian-inspired armchairs.

ABOVE: A Chinese-red bamboo games table serves as command central in this living room and complements sunny yellow curtains and chartreuse walls. RIGHT: First and foremost, buy what you love—as evidenced by my own Newport, Rhode Island, living room. A Japanese screen adds interest to a long wall, a bamboo étagère provides a home for favorite books and antique porcelain, old-fashioned slipcovers with a ruffled edge look fresh against an antique rug, and Chinese fretwork chairs lacquered red are a welcome respite from the beloved blue throughout my home.

ABOVE: Antiques are even more appreciated when mixed with the contemporary, and old chinoiserie lamps and vintage brass boxes add a wonderful collected look. OPPOSITE: A custom Greek-key application on tailored Roman shades provide a note of modernity in this turn-of-the-century house. FOLLOWING SPREAD: Every chair is an opportunity to make a fun statement.

RIGHT: Modern art brings everything up to date and tells a story—one large painting offers great scale and balance, especially over a generous three-cushion sofa. Metal faux-bois chairs, lacquered side tables, and an exotic grain–painted coffee table continue the contemporary feel.

FOLLOWING SPREAD: Straw and brass complement the new upholstery on a cozy custom banquette. Blue trim along the bottom of a brown sofa lightens the effect, and a jute rug from India keeps the look Southampton casual.

For an old-world paneled library in a 1920s home, finishing touches include a turn-of-the-century lamp, elegant hurricanes, and a large Regency mirror.

ABOVE: An antique alabaster lamp atop a vintage Chinese bamboo console draws the eye toward architectural windows. Chairs in an interesting mix of styles keep furnishings from looking too paired off. OPPOSITE: Cabinetry painted the same high-gloss finish as the walls keeps this small library cohesive. Your eye can't help but be drawn to the large midcentury painting and the great mix of pillows and accessories.

Keeping the majority of a room neutral allows you to periodically update your finishing touches. Save the riskier fabric for a smaller piece that's easier to update if the pizzazz fades. Antique chairs and little benches create flexible spaces that make conversation easy. Thanks to a variety of side tables, every seat has a place to put down a glass.

OPPOSITE: Feel happy in your home from the moment you arrive. A beautiful antique brass door knocker and a nineteenth-century Louis Philippe console are welcoming elements. ABOVE LEFT: It's a simple trifecta for a front hall: a lamp is warmer than overhead light, greenery from the garden or the corner market makes a space feel lived in, and one can never have enough catchall trays. ABOVE RIGHT: A more exotic option for the front hall is an antique Anglo-Indian settee—an eclectic mix of pillows and a small picture hung above go a long way in making this oft-neglected space feel finished and welcoming.

OPPOSITE: A back hallway is an ideal place for an attractive bench that functions perfectly for taking off shoes or dropping a bag. The addition of an antique rug lends age to a newly renovated home, and large-scale artwork balances the tall ceilings. ABOVE: An oak-paneled mudroom is a casual yet visually pleasing nook for coats, boots, and book bags. A forgiving rug that withstands trampling helps to protect the aged terra-cotta floors.

RIGHT: What truly gives a room longevity is classic, comfortable upholstery. Instead of a silky sofa one might slip off of, choose materials that feel good. Intriguing antique Regency planters, little ceramic pots, and antique bowls are interesting holders for plants and flowers.

FOLLOWING SPREAD: Only a few objects need to catch the eye, such as these antique porcelain lamps that flank a sofa and a large Chinese wallpaper panel with a gilded-bamboo frame. The only other touches you need are beautiful pillows, fresh flowers, and the unexpected twist of a pair of tiger-print chairs.

HOWARD MILLER LIBRARY
ZEELAND, MI 49464

ABOVE: When in doubt, Chinese antiques, such as this pair of antique bone pagodas that flank a European oil painting, add warmth and character. Flowers in wicker votives tone down the formality of a marble mantel. OPPOSITE: Finishing touches are a way to keep a space looking fresh. Every so often, edit and rotate objets d'art so you'll appreciate each item more. A mix of old and new enliven and balance each room.

Gracious Dining

WHILE MY DINNER PREPARATIONS TEND TO BE SIMPLE AND UNCOMPLICATED, MY STRONG SUIT IS SETTING THE TABLE. Before guests arrive, I like to experiment with various soup bowls and serving pieces or play around with various arrangements of flowers. Regardless of whether the resulting table setting is a masterpiece or a rough draft, I truly enjoy those rare quiet creative moments. Much like decorating, entertaining is a skill you can improve with practice, so revel in your mistakes and have fun.

IT'S INHERENTLY SOUTHERN TO VALUE THE COMFORT OF YOUR GUESTS ABOVE ALL ELSE. This is especially important in a traditionally formal space like the dining room that's tailor-made for entertaining. Well-thought-out design can have a big impact on your guests' mood, and simplicity is the key to keeping things from getting too fussy. For instance, the trick to entertaining with your grandmother's china is to add something a little organic and modern, like green cabbage plates layered on top for the first course. It gives the composition a youthful but elegant face-lift. Or try mixing bamboo flatware or rattan chargers with the good silver. Your grandmother would approve!

WHILE THE DINING ROOM IS PERHAPS MOST ASSOCIATED WITH HOLIDAYS, IT WOULD BE A MISSTEP TO DESIGN ENTIRELY AROUND THE ANNUAL THANKSGIVING OR CHRISTMAS GATHERING. Anticipate how to accommodate different scenarios or party sizes, and give yourself options. Think about how you enjoy spending time with family and friends. If you host a large annual Easter dinner, consider a table that can be extended with leaves but still works for your smaller weekly Sunday supper for four. Personally, I love small dinners during the winter and buffet-style meals in the summer. In Newport, Rhode Island, my magic number is about thirty guests. I seat twelve at my round table in the dining room, ten in the breakfast room, and eight on the adjacent terrace connecting to the breakfast room. I always keep the seating charts to remember who sat where so I can mix things up the next time.

KEEP IN MIND A SENSE OF PLACE: EVERY DINING ROOM IS SET UP A BIT DIFFERENTLY AND HAS A DIFFERENT PURPOSE. If you must pass through the dining room to get to the kitchen, it should have a lighter daytime feel. A dining room set off on its own can carry a more dramatic evening ambience. Regardless, first consider how you'll use the space and build in some flexibility. If you don't have a

separate breakfast room, you may want the dining room to hit cheerful notes for lunch or brunch. Or it might double as a creatively stimulating space where you spread out to write or study—it doesn't need to be just for special occasions.

IT'S IMPORTANT TO HAVE STORAGE FOR CHINA, CHAMPAGNE FLUTES, AND SILVERWARE IN A DINING ROOM OR A PANTRY CLOSE BY, WHETHER THAT'S A PIECE OF FURNITURE OR PIVOT-HINGE CLOSETS THAT COMPLETELY DISAPPEAR BEHIND WALLPAPER. Think of it as an accessories closet—a place to keep finishing touches like vases at your fingertips and make arranging your own flowers feel more celebratory, even if you're just picking up roses from the market. Especially if you entertain more than a few times a year, consider what you might need and assemble a go-to kit you can tuck away for last-minute use. I have a supply of inexpensive ballroom chairs and bamboo flatware stored in a closet for my larger parties, so I never have to bother with rentals.

GOING BACK TO THE COMFORT FACTOR: ANTIQUE CHAIRS CAN BE LOVELY, BUT IF YOU WANT PEOPLE TO SIT AND STAY AWHILE, I'M MORE INCLINED TOWARD UPHOLSTERED CHAIRS. New dining chairs and an old table make a compelling combination. Just remember that the fabric should be forgiving—you don't want to ever be upset that someone spilled a little sauce. If you don't have a dining table that you adore, a pretty skirted tablecloth is a great option. As an added bonus, it helps absorb sound.

HAVING A FOCAL POINT IN THE DINING ROOM, WHETHER IT'S A STRIKING PIECE OF ART OR DRAMATIC CHANDELIER, IS GROUNDING AND ADDS A SENSE OF INTIMACY. This is one room where you can be a bit more over the top than one normally would. Remember, a dining room is a gift—not everyone has one, so you should enjoy it and share it. We're all so busy, it's easy to go out to dinner or plop down in the kitchen. But getting into the habit of using your dining room sets a nice standard for your home. When my kids come home from boarding school or we have houseguests, I always make the effort to do something special, and these evenings often become some of our fondest memories. Take out the pretty plates you don't use every day, and sit down together. This space is about celebrating and having some fun.

OPPOSITE: A white-painted Parsons table, rattan chairs, and white vinyl banquette lighten up a sunny breakfast room. The tropical-print curtains give the space an airy coastal feel. FOLLOWING SPREAD, LEFT: Heirloom chairs reupholstered in a teal velvet and chartreuse walls with a bit of gloss add a youthful pop to a traditional and verdant dining room. FOLLOWING SPREAD, RIGHT: To create a welcoming table, experiment with varying styles of china. Cabbage-leaf plates mix beautifully with more traditional patterns.

It sounds counterintuitive, but in a room with little natural light, darker colors are more successful— here, rich green velvet hung like wallpaper is alive with drama. Equally at home are antiques: a French dining table, English chairs and sideboard, and a chinoiserie screen complement the existing antique rug. Above all, a dining room should feel gracious and hospitable, and a pair of ceramic fish adds a lively touch to the formal tabletop.

ABOVE: To add a sense of history, antique Caldwell sconces hang above a George III marble-topped gold-leafed antique console, a useful serving piece.
RIGHT: Simplicity in palette keeps a grand space from feeling too fussy. Silver damask wallpaper keeps a pass-through dining room neutral and sunny—it's equally pretty by day or night. To accommodate large gatherings, the rectangular dining table with leaves seats up to two dozen guests. New chairs covered in velvet with leather seats keep the room from feeling antiquated.

ABOVE AND OPPOSITE: A favorite pairing of ochre yellow and Chinese orange reads very warm in this dining room, and sets the scene for some fabulous dinner parties. Lattice wallpaper with white paneling below, a cozy skirted round table, and rattan chairs are chic without being too serious. A simple Indian jute rug takes the edge off all the color.

OPPOSITE: An informal dining room off the kitchen invites guests to sit and stay awhile with the addition of cushy upholstered chairs and a wool dhurrie. The scale and impact of a whimsical light fixture and the sleek slab of a lacquered-wood table bring a modern look to a traditional home. ABOVE: Simplicity is chic. The warmth of a home's decor continues to an outdoor dining terrace off the kitchen, where classic blue and white linens add flair to a teak table and chairs. Assemble a collection of interesting vases to have on hand—even simple flowers from the garden turn the everyday into a celebration.

ABOVE: An essential bar space becomes midcentury cool: The mirrored and lacquered bar of an informal dining room provides a wonderful nook to display colorful glassware and conceal appliances. OPPOSITE: Sea Island, Georgia, is all about the view of the water, and a sharp blue-and-white dining room feels like an extension of the ocean. Curtains frame the windows but don't distract from the vista, and a custom linen-wrapped table adds lovely subtle texture when guests sit down to dine. A striking oil on canvas provides an additional focal point and references the home's surroundings.

OPPOSITE: An inviting breakfast room gets a dose of yellow and green cheer that reflects the morning sunlight. Forgivable vinyl seat cushions that withstand spills and a built-in cabinet to accommodate dining necessities play to a large family's need for practicality. ABOVE: Much like decorating, gracious entertaining is a skill that improves by cheerful experimentation with different combinations of place settings.

ABOVE: There are many ways to make gatherings of different sizes work. At my family's lake house, part of the great room is dedicated to a grand old table for eighteen built many years ago—it goes on forever, thanks to added leaves. It's the perfect place to play with casual table settings. OPPOSITE: Dining outdoors can be just as elegant as dining indoors. Metal outdoor furniture on a charming guesthouse porch in Jamaica withstands the elements and provides a picturesque setting. A vintage scalloped tole sconce lends a subtle 1960s flair.

Cheerful Kitchens and Baths

I SIMPLY CANNOT RESIST A CLASSIC, CRISP WHITE KITCHEN. WITHOUT FAIL, IT PROVIDES A GREAT BASE OF OPERATION THAT FEELS CLEAN, FRESH, AND CONDUCIVE TO COOKING. The kitchen is often the heart of a home, and a universally agreeable white backdrop provides a beautiful blank slate for this gathering place to take on a personality of its own through finishing touches. Cabinets painted soft white, a porcelain sink that creates a sense of fluidity with pristine countertops, and a simply shaped hood are neutral but dynamic focal points—it's my philosophy that one only needs a few standout details in a room for it to have great impact. To punctuate a monochromatic kitchen I'm always longing for a dose of color and pattern, and the energetic punch of a mosaic-tile backsplash, bold upholstered barstools, or cheerful colored placemats pulls together the space and helps it feel finished.

BUILDING A FEW SURPRISES INTO A KITCHEN'S SCHEMATIC LAYOUT, LIKE PAINTING THE INSIDE OF GLASS-FRONTED CABINETS AN INTRIGUING COLOR, BECOMES A LITTLE TREAT EVERY TIME YOU REACH FOR YOUR PLATES. Not only will such well-chosen details add a bit of color, but they can also help to soften the effect of a kitchen's dominant harder-edged wood, glass, and stone surfaces. As I write, I am designing my own white kitchen with a high-gloss blue tray ceiling and a subtle blue leopard wallpaper that does a fabulous job connecting the ceiling and walls. I absolutely love it.

IF YOUR HOME LACKS SPACE FOR A SEPARATE BREAKFAST ROOM, TRY DRESSING UP YOUR ISLAND. Often a kitchen's command central, islands make a great focal point that can lure the whole family to pile in for breakfast. To make an island conducive to such gatherings as well as family meals, add great-looking comfortable barstools and an impactful light fixture above.

I LOVE AN OLD-FASHIONED QUALITY IN A HOUSE, AND A TRADITIONAL BUTLER'S PANTRY CAN OFFER THAT KIND OF WARMTH WITH ORGANIZED LAYERS OF INTEREST. The square footage typically is not grand, but this room has immense opportunity for style—here is where you can incorporate that dynamic wallpaper or light fixture you're dying to use, but which might be too intimidating in a more visible area of your home. These indulgent details can elevate a small space into a decorated room that's integral to entertaining.

SIMILAR TO THE PANTRY, THE POWDER ROOM IS ANOTHER PLACE WHERE IT PAYS TO BE EMPHATICALLY WHIMSICAL. Functionality is more important in other baths that are used daily. Feel free to take risks and infuse this space with personality. Since it's a place you won't see too often, it certainly should never be boring. Dare I say, it can even be a little out there. I like to see how far clients are willing to go, gently guiding them toward fanciful chinoiserie or a lacquered vanity—the choices made here speak volumes about one's personality.

EVEN THE MOST CONSERVATIVE HOME CAN PUSH THE DESIGN OF A POWDER ROOM TO THE EDGE. One client moving to a beautiful home in Locust Valley, New York, was leaving the city apartment she inherited from her parents, where her mother had commissioned the talented illustrator Hilary Knight (of Eloise fame) to paint the powder room. Luckily, the artwork was done on canvas, so we could carefully remove it and install it in her new house. When we were done, we even threw a little cocktail party in celebration of this uniquely original space. It continues to be a lovely surprise for anyone who walks in for the first time.

THINK ABOUT HOW YOU CAN MAKE A ROOM'S EXPERIENCE UNIQUE. As a lover of antiques, I'm always looking for pieces that can be repurposed as powder-room vanities. For example, undermount a sink and faucet into a Chinese cabinet, or upgrade an ordinary vanity with interesting hardware to make it feel more custom. The sink in my Newport powder room is an Asian altar table with a honed-slate top and undermount sink—it's the perfect size, and it adds so much character to the quirky space. In a powder room, details make all the difference. Guests will remember these beautiful and thoughtful additions.

With the right details, a small bar takes on the feel of an entertaining space rather than a standard kitchen. Cabinetry painted a dynamic blue and Meg Braff Designs Nanking chinoiserie wallpaper offer a glamorous profile, and adding mercury glass to the facade allows light to bounce around the space.

A classic neutral kitchen is low-commitment because everything works with everything—simply changing one or two details will give it a whole new look. Asian-influenced wooden stools tuck away under the island's practical Caesarstone countertops. Natural materials like wood and straw warm up the room and, more importantly, are highly functional and practical. Unlined matchstick shades don't absorb kitchen odors and are easy to wipe down if someone touches them with cooking oil.

ABOVE: The patina and beautiful color of Chinese Chippendale chairs add a little whimsy to a breakfast room and blend well with a simple farm table; seat cushions make it all the more comfortable. OPPOSITE: The graphic scale of a great wallpaper can truly transform a small, ordinary kitchen. A banquette upholstered in chocolate brown vinyl adds practicality to white Saarinen-style chairs.

A mosaic backsplash of Moroccan cement tiles adds texture
and graphic interest so the kitchen feels unique. A fun rattan
light fixture and low-slung barstools in washable lime
vinyl leather jazz up but don't overwhelm the double island.

ABOVE: It can be challenging to fit a console on a curved wall—instead, a rolling bar cart offers great flexibility and provides a place to set up juice or coffee. OPPOSITE: Dramatic green leaf-print wallpaper in a window-filled breakfast room connects with the outdoors and gives a conservatory-like feel to the space—the wallpaper tapers toward the ceiling to conceal the room's slightly awkward shape. A Saarinen table with rattan chairs and a round jute rug add warmth.

To keep a dining room's focus on its water views, decoration should be kept minimal. An all-white room—white walls, white curtains, white Karl Springer–style table, white-lacquered floors—gives a late-1960s vibe. Brightly upholstered chairs, a vintage Gio Ponti brass chandelier, and a contemporary abstract painting liven up the space. Large ceramic seashells on the table reference the ocean outside.

164

OPPOSITE: My Meadow Reed wallpaper envelops a square dining room overlooking Long Island Sound. Chartreuse trim complements the wallpaper, so the room reads as a cohesive space. An existing table base painted white and paired with chairs upholstered in a outdoor fabric gives the light-filled space a crisp, clean new life.
ABOVE: A modern white kitchen's textural floor runner is a nice layer underfoot. One large piece of art pulls in the colors from the family room just beyond. Hotel silver displayed in the pantry adds a bit of sparkle.

OPPOSITE AND ABOVE: Turquoise tilework is a beautiful pop of color against the classic all-white kitchen. In a beach house, where life is a bit simpler, crisp white open shelves to display dishes keep the look light and bright.

ABOVE: Cabinetry painted deep red, custom-colored wallpaper, and brass hardware add richness to a bar space set up for entertaining. OPPOSITE: The forest green and sage butler's pantry in an old-world Colonial Revival home feels like a little jewel box next to the kitchen. A simple patterned wallpaper and antique rugs on the floor add charming age to the gleaming new mahogany counters and unlacquered-brass fittings.

RIGHT: Similar to a classic white kitchen, an all-white bath benefits from the energetic punch of a single, strong color. A lively dose of yellow in artwork and accessories adds a modern jolt and softens the harder surfaces. FOLLOWING SPREAD: Lively wallpaper can shake a staid bath out of its slumber and distracts the eye from a room with a quirky shape. In a tiny powder room, a mirror in a slender frame in proportion with the sink can make the space look larger without weighing it down. Antique furniture reimagined as a vanity is a nice departure from mundane cabinetry. A bath with natural light lends itself to a lighter background; if there is no window, a darker color offers a little release.

Pretty Bedrooms

IN THE BEDROOM, MY BEST ADVICE IS TO KEEP IT PRETTY. Gorgeous new monogrammed linens paired with lovely antique bedside tables and deliciously soft carpeting underfoot is my idea of heaven. In a way, the bedroom should be the most beautiful room in your home because it's often where you spend the most time, so decorate it in a way that invites you to linger for a while. This private and personal space should be soothing, restful, and harmonious. More than anything, it should be a place you dream of waking up in.

KEEP SIMPLICITY IN MIND—IN THE BEDROOM, DESIGN NEED NOT BE OVERLY COMPLICATED. It's more impactful to focus on one main statement with a little scale and presence, so let those colors and patterns dictate your choices. Maybe you've fallen in love with the hue and pattern of a beautiful wallpaper. You might initially think it's too much, but in the end the widespread color will almost read as a neutral. For my own bedroom in Palm Beach, I found a fanciful Asian-inspired pink wallpaper that also feels sophisticated and mature. Fittingly, the color creates a sense of calm and peace of mind. Plus, with four sons and a husband, I felt I deserved a touch of femininity!

THERE IS SOMETHING WELCOMING AND APPROACHABLE ABOUT TRADITIONAL DECORATING IN THIS PARTICULAR SPACE. To bring order and balance, make use of symmetrical arrangements. Well-mannered pairs of lamps or nightstands in the master bedroom, twin beds or bookshelves in a child's room, or two luggage stands or chairs in a guest room offer flexibility and a sense of continuity. The doubling effect creates a polish that's pleasing to the eye.

ANYONE WHO HAS VISITED MY STORE CAN ATTEST TO MY PASSION FOR UNUSUAL BENCHES AND STOOLS. I'm constantly buying them because they are so useful, especially in the bedroom, to put up your feet, stack books, place a breakfast tray, or tuck into a vanity or at the foot of a bed as an extra seat.

HOWARD MILLER LIBRARY
ZEELAND, MI 49464

CUSTOMIZING A FEW KEY ITEMS TIPS A SPACE TOWARD A MORE ARTFUL AND CHIC AESTHETIC, AND MONOGRAMMED BEDDING IS THE LOVELIEST FINISHING TOUCH. Investing in quality custom linens with a high thread count pulls together a bedroom and keeps everything looking neat and uniform. Plus, climbing into luxurious sheets at night makes you feel special. I pretty much insist that every client order one great set for each bedroom.

FOR A BEDROOM THAT LEANS TOWARD THE MONOCHROMATIC, CUSTOM FABRIC OR LACQUERED LAMPSHADES ARE A GREAT WAY TO ADD PUNCH AND FINISH. It's an ideal moment to layer in a personalized piece, and the beautiful glaze adds a reflective quality that catches your eye against more patterned and textured fabrics.

DESKTOPS ARE ANOTHER OPPORTUNITY FOR BEAUTY AND A FLEXIBLE SPACE THAT CAN BE UNIQUELY YOURS IN THE BEDROOM. Most of all, the desk should reflect your needs and feel connected to the rest of the room. The essentials: shelves or a bookcase to display books or sentimental items and maximize vertical space above the desk's surface; baskets to keep things neat and tidy and a drawer to tuck things away. If you're more of a lip gloss than a laptop type of person, a desk can also be used as a dressing table or vanity—just hang a mirror instead of a memo board. Since my husband and I share a bathroom in Newport, I use our dressing-room desk as another station to put on makeup or dry my hair before an evening out.

PUTTING A LITTLE TIME AND ORGANIZATION INTO YOUR BEDROOM'S DRESSING SPACE CAN TRULY TRANSFORM THE EXPERIENCE. I prefer closets that can be closed and present a more polished effect. Functionality is important, but a closet doesn't have to be custom; something as inexpensive as a repurposed mirrored credenza glams it up more than typical shelving and cabinets (for my own closet in Florida, the cabinetry came from a thrift shop). If you have space for a real dressing room or walk-in closet, consider covering the walls with wallpaper or a pretty paint color to make the room as rich and inviting as your favorite boutique.

The bedroom is often where you spend the most time, so make it extra beautiful.
A lighthearted pink space offers a sense of serenity, and wallpaper in a fanciful Asian design from Quadrille blankets the room with a feminine yet sophisticated feel.

Simplicity in a palette is restful in a bedroom. A shallow scalloped valance conceals the curtain hardware and is a smart option for a room with low ceilings.

OPPOSITE: The geometry of a circular pattern beautifully mirrors—quite literally—the trellis pattern of a love seat. The bedroom is the home's most personal space, so incorporate only the elements you love, like a vintage rattan ottoman painted white or an upholstered Parsons chair. ABOVE: Repurposed drawers found at a thrift shop prettified with Lucite pulls organize and transform an otherwise ordinary closet.

ABOVE AND OPPOSITE: Less is more, and a bedroom should above all feel soothing and easy on the eye. A repetition of three fabrics—white, a solid color, and a complementary pattern—unifies the decor. Extra seating, like a bench at the foot of the bed and a comfortable chaise, are restful places to put up your feet. A pair of large side tables provides ample space for books and trinkets.

PREVIOUS SPREAD: Soft blue strikes a balance, creating an ambience that's neither overtly masculine nor feminine. Paired with crisp white, it's serene without feeling too saccharine. ABOVE: Bedroom furnishings can serve multiple purposes. A Jansen table doubles as a writing desk or dressing table, and the oval mirror above it softens the space. OPPOSITE, CLOCKWISE FROM TOP LEFT: Custom monogrammed bedding brings a beautiful old-fashioned touch. Ceramic lamps are a staple thanks to their range of outgoing colors and organic shapes. A simple white vase on a nightstand offers an element of nature. Benches are useful in any room, for dropping shopping bags, or putting on shoes.

ABOVE: A pair of heirloom twin beds find new life with fresh bedding and blankets; a hard-won swordfish trophy surveys the scene from above. The small room lacks desk space, but you can still incorporate one as a bedside table with a chair. OPPOSITE: Once again, an old-fashioned antique bed is a beautiful showpiece when paired with a modern graphic bed skirt and an Alexander Calder lithograph, which offer a snappy outlook in a young boy's room.

Pairs rule in this beachy Jamaica bedroom.
Symmetry is at play in bedside tables, lamps, and
benches, so the overall effect is easy on the eye. In
this guest room, the twin beds can either be
nestled together or separated for more flexibility.
The Caribbean calls for less upholstery, so rattan
headboards feel right at home. As a finishing touch,
a breezy striped rug lightens dark wood floors.

ABOVE: In a home where every bedroom is blue, a teenage girl's private space is distinguished by playful pops of color on curtains, a theme that's repeated throughout the room. A generous dose of bamboo and white lacquer rattan keep the effect fun and youthful. OPPOSITE: Stripes used horizontally add a modern touch. A turquoise sisal carpet provides texture against crisp cotton beds.

OPPOSITE: Natural materials are chic and tone down the formality of a bedroom. A Chinese-inspired fretwork lattice print and custom bamboo bed linens add charm in the Caribbean. A straw rug crafted by a local artisan weaves in regional flavor. ABOVE: A similar yellow takes on an entirely new feel on an upholstered platform bed and batik coverlet in Southampton. A mix of old and new—a modern lacquered side table paired with a vintage rattan stool—gives the room restful layers of interest.

ABOVE: Paint truly transforms a space, and offbeat colors are equally eye-catching in the bedroom. A daybed with a gathered skirt conceals a trundle bed, perfect for sleepovers in a teenage girl's bedroom. Colorful framed art and graphic patterns repeated throughout add a modern touch.
OPPOSITE: Another way to add color is with painted furniture. This blue lacquered chest of drawers is both modern and timeless, and provides contrast to the chartreuse walls.

One outstanding detail really makes a monochromatic green bedroom. Here, the curtains are the showstopper, adding pattern and interest. A modern upholstered chair with a contrasting white frame provides comfy seating without weighing down the room.

ABOVE: In a large bedroom, the subtle and soft graphic element of one consistent fabric repeated on walls, curtains, and furnishings unifies the space. While decorating is more intuitive than formulaic, graphic prints tend to make upholstered chairs and pleated bed skirts a little less buttoned-up and more breezy. On a vast king-sized bed, monogrammed bedding is a special luxury that truly stands out. OPPOSITE: In all of its forms, classic blue and white has a universally wonderful, airy feeling and appeals to both men and women.

PREVIOUS SPREAD: Pale lavender walls are a perfect complement to the range of purple hues incorporated into a young girl's bedroom. ABOVE: A desk placed near a bedroom window with the great asset of abundant natural light is all the more conducive to sitting—straw shades are ideal to add color and filter the light. OPPOSITE: Small details, such as a Chinese pagoda–style lacquered mirror or modern Lucite chair, add impact and make these desks enviable spots to settle in for primping or writing.

PREVIOUS SPREAD: Custom upholstered wooden headboards add remarkable geometry, scale, and color to a small bedroom. Coral linen leopard-print curtains and a striped rug pull together the scheme in one swoop—it's upbeat and sassy. ABOVE AND OPPOSITE: A monochromatic blue bedroom achieves maximum drama with my Sporting d'Ete wallpaper, faux-bois bedside tables, and elegant custom linens. Just about anything can be beautified with wallpaper, including a lacquered desk. A custom rug from India adds a geometric counterpoint.

ABOVE: White lacquer, vintage brass, gold-tasseled sconces, and a white plaster mirror add charm and glamour to a windowless dressing room. OPPOSITE: A closet with doors that close helps keep a dressing space looking tidy. The interior of the closet is wallpapered, offering a lovely surprise each time you open the door.

Outdoor Style

I SAVOR RELAXED MOMENTS IN THE OPEN AIR. IT'S HOW MY EXTENDED FAMILY ENTERTAINS AT OUR SUMMER HOME ON PICKWICK LAKE IN MISSISSIPPI. My grandmother designed a table for our indoor/outdoor great room that's been the setting of many memorable family dinners over the past seventy years. The long, rustic wooden table expands to seat eighteen, but whether it's six or eighteen for dinner, it never feels like a lot of effort. When the party starts to grow, the local ribs place caters and Mom adds in her special dishes, served on attractive paper plates that keep cleanup to a stress-free minimum. After dinner, there are always s'mores and often a sunset boat ride.

OUTDOOR SPACES HAVE BECOME INTEGRAL TO PRESENT-DAY LIFE AND DICTATE A LEVEL OF ATTENTION FORMERLY RESERVED FOR INTERIORS. Creating this enriching "extra room" should be as pleasurable as designing your interiors. Think of your ideal outdoor space as an extension of your home where you will dine, entertain, read, enjoy the garden, or admire the view—and how it can be made unique to your family. For example, while I love a good barbecue, I'm also toying with the idea of a hibachi table for my outdoor terrace area in Locust Valley. I picture my husband, sons, and I all pulling on our fleeces and cozying up to an easy dinner of grilled steak and vegetables on a crisp fall evening.

THE GOAL FOR A SUCCESSFUL OUTDOOR ROOM IS AN ORGANIC AESTHETIC THAT FLOWS SEAMLESSLY FROM THE INSIDE AND DOESN'T DISTRACT FROM THE PICTURESQUE SURROUNDINGS. For a project on the laid-back, beachy banks of North Carolina, we created a protected outdoor room on the lower level of the house with comfortable seating, dining, an outdoor fireplace, and a Ping-Pong table. Outdoor showers and changing rooms are close by for convenience after a swim in the ocean, and there is even a little bunk room and bathroom for extra sleepover guests. It is one of the most enjoyable spaces I have designed.

TO CREATE AN EASY TRANSITION BETWEEN INSIDE AND OUT, HAVE THE STYLE MIMIC THE INTERIOR, BUT LET IT BE LESS DECORATED, LOOSENED UP, AND EASY ON THE EYE. For larger furnishings, I'm drawn to solid-colored upholstery, and I reserve heavier patterns for smaller pillows or table settings—that way, you can take it away or change it a little for variety. While it's a staple in my repertoire, a blue-and-green scheme lends itself particularly well to the colors of nature and blends beautifully in the sunlight. If a blue living room leads to a lovely veranda, perhaps the alfresco space features beige seat cushions with blue piping that references the indoors. Terrific pops of color—bold pink, orange, or yellow—whether on a bright oversize umbrella, an outdoor rug, or a set of tumblers, can also bring enormous energy to a landscape. Easy outdoor style requires low-maintenance accessories: cheerful striped cotton rugs, durable indoor/outdoor fabrics, and streamlined furniture. Certain materials make for a better marriage in the open air, like teak with rattan to give a modern midcentury feel, or simple wicker and outdoor sisal to keep the atmosphere casual. Whatever your aesthetic, make sure it is practical.

OUTDOOR ENTERTAINING IS A FULL SENSORY EXPERIENCE AND CAN BE AS CASUAL OR COMPLEX AS YOU CHOOSE. Just like your family room, you'll need a place to set down a drink or put up your feet, so include a generous coffee table or colorful ceramic garden stools. A screened porch might be a necessity in an area prone to mosquitoes. Sun protection is also an absolute must, and there are many ways to think about shade on a terrace. One of the easiest and most flexible ways to provide it is via one huge umbrella or multiple smaller ones. An awning offers great flexibility—it can be permanent with material that gets taken down in the winter or is retractable. I'm a big proponent of creating a classic metal arbor dressed up with entwined vines. And of course you need lights. Have outdoor sconces and lighting on dimmers, or a lantern and stash of hurricanes on hand to illuminate the table come sunset.

JUST AS YOU EXPERIMENT WITH CHINA IN THE DINING ROOM, GIVE YOURSELF FREE REIN OVER ACCESSORIES OUTDOORS. A tablecloth, rather than place mats, often lends itself to the environment because it softens the look of more minimal upholstery. Inexpensive yet attractive acrylic cups, tumblers, and trays are ideal for serving drinks and appetizers. My favorites are melamine and bamboo.

EVEN IN THE OFF-SEASON, IT'S FUN TO HAVE SOMETHING TO DO OUTDOORS. An outdoor fireplace or fire pit is always a big hit. Our good friends in Newport are known for their pizza oven, a universally appealing idea that brings everyone outdoors even when it's chilly. And a bar is a key feature for outdoor parties, whether it's a summer barbecue or an early spring soiree when guests are itching to take a breather under the stars.

In Palm Beach, a majestic open loggia with eleven-foot ceilings and pecky cypress beams is a welcoming oasis leading to the pool and garden designed by landscape architect Mario Nievera. A blue-and-green backdrop especially lends itself to the colors of nature and blends beautifully with the strong Florida sunlight.

RIGHT: Old-world rattan furniture placed alongside a traditional home's columns frames the view from a quaint covered porch with a herringbone brick terrace. FOLLOWING SPREAD: Rattan and teak furniture paired with a locally made rug create an organic, indoor/outdoor decorative moment on an inviting loggia designed for lounging. A large hexagonal mirror captures the natural light flowing through this small Jamaica cottage.

LEFT: Outdoor fabrics in subtle neutral patterns are forgiving and habitually chic. A streamlined sectional sofa and cheerful striped rug ground the seating area. In lieu of a typical side table, a white ceramic garden stool adds a little shine. FOLLOWING SPREAD: Woven outdoor furniture with aqua cushions is a go-to combination that feels at one with nature in a Southern beach house. A picnic-style table and custom benches support a large family's casual lifestyle—it's all about the view and the company here.

The ideal outdoor space is an extension of your home in which you dine, entertain, or read. It's lucky that every metal bamboo-style chair on the second-floor terrace has a spectacular view of this North Carolina marsh. A straw rug blends with the wood-planked floor and adds a little texture underfoot. A bar cart just off the bedroom inside allows easy access to morning coffee or an evening nightcap.

RIGHT: Aluminum rattan-style furniture withstands the elements on this Caribbean porch. Solid-colored fabric on the furniture is a timeless choice because it doesn't compete with the surroundings. A small gesture of patterned pillows adds a pop of personality and can be changed seasonally or whenever the mood strikes. FOLLOWING SPREAD: Custom NanaWall glass doors provide a seamless transition between the inside of a modern pool house and the backyard, where a large dining table provides ample seating for family gatherings.

Comfortable rattan seating and an outdoor bar make a porch off a library an inviting retreat for curling up with a book. The outdoor aesthetic should be an extension of the indoors, but let it be less decorated, more loosened up, and easy on the eye.

ABOVE: On Long Island, an inviting outdoor space can be as casual or complex as you like. An additional small dining table off the breakfast room is an alternative space in which to enjoy an alfresco morning meal. OPPOSITE: A simple French country vibe on a new outdoor deck in a 1960s house complements the view of the marsh on Sea Island.

Resources

ANTIQUES

1stdibs Showroom
200 Lexington Avenue
New York, NY 10016
(646) 293-6633
1stdibs.com/nydc/

The Antique and Artisan Gallery
69 Jefferson Street
Stamford, CT 06902
(203) 327-6022
antiqueandartisan.com

Doyle
175 East 87th Street
New York, NY 10128
(212) 427-4141
doyle.com
Multiple locations

Elizabeth Pash Antiques &
Decoration
94 Forest Avenue
Locust Valley, NY 11560
(516) 277-1551
elizabethpash.com

Harbor View Center for Antiques
101 Jefferson Street
Stamford, CT 06902
(203) 325-8070
harborviewantiques.com

Hiden Galleries
47 John Street
Stamford, CT 06902
(203) 363-0003
hidengalleries.com

John Rosselli & Associates
979 Third Avenue,
Suite 1800
New York, NY 10022
(212) 593-2060
johnrosselli.com
Multiple locations

Meg Braff Designs
92 Forest Avenue
Locust Valley, NY 11560
(516) 801-4939
megbraffdesigns.com

Palm Beach Antique and
Design Center
6910 South Dixie Highway
West Palm Beach, FL 33405
(561) 588-5868
palmbeachantique.com

STAIR Auctioneers and
Appraisers
549 Warren Street
Hudson, NY 12534
(518) 751-1000
stairgalleries.com

ART

Christie's
20 Rockefeller Plaza
New York, NY 10020
(212) 636-2000
christies.com
Multiple locations

Soicher Marin
7245 16th Street East, Suite 110
Sarasota, FL 34243
(941) 308-7500
soicher-marin.com

Sotheby's New York
1334 York Avenue
New York, NY 10021
(212) 606-7000
sothebys.com
Multiple locations

Wendover Art Group
wendoverart.com

BATHROOMS

Ann Sacks
204 East 58th Street
New York, NY 10022
(212) 588-1920
annsacks.com
Multiple locations

Kohler
kohler.com

Newport Brass
newportbrass.com

P. E. Guerin
23 Jane Street
New York, NY 10014
(212) 243-5270
peguerin.com

Waterworks
215 East 58th Street
New York, NY 10022
(212) 371-9266
waterworks.com
Multiple locations

CARPETS

Country Carpet & Rug
207 Robbins Lane
Syosset, NY 11791
(516) 822-5855
countrycarpet.com

Dash & Albert
125 Pecks Road
Pittsfield, MA 01201
(877) 586 4771
dashandalbert.com

L & M Custom Carpets and Rugs
lmcustomcarpets.com

Magdelena York Collection
MagdalenaYorkCollection.com

Stark
979 Third Avenue, 11th Floor
New York, NY 10022
(844) 40-STARK
starkcarpet.com
Multiple locations

CASE GOODS

Bungalow 5
251 West 30th Street, Suite 10W
New York, NY 10001
(212) 947-1500
bungalow5.com
Multiple locations

Century Furniture
centuryfurniture.com

Henredon
henredon.com

Hickory Chair
hickorychair.com

Interlude
interludehome.com

Made Goods
madegoods.com

Matthews & Parker
matthewsandparker.com

Mr. Brown
New York Showroom
200 Lexington Avenue,
#604
New York, NY 10016
(646) 293-6622
mrbrownlondon.com

Palecek
200 Lexington Ave, Suite 610
New York, NY 10016
(212) 287-0063
palecek.com
Multiple locations

Selamat
selamatdesigns.com

CURTAINS

Barbara Barry
www.kravet.com/products/
collections/barbara-barry/

Gonsman Drapery & Upholstery
(561) 732-8841

Morgik Metal Designs
145 Hudson Street
New York, NY 10013
(212) 463-0304
morgik.com

Ona Drapery Hardware
onadrapery.com

Ray Goodman
(516) 238-0493

FABRICS AND WALLCOVERINGS

Bernard Thorp
53 Chelsea Manor Street
SW3 5RZ
London, United Kingdom
+44 (0) 20 7352 5745
bernardthorp.co.uk

Bob Collins & Sons, Inc.
bobcollinsandsons.com

Brunschwig & Fils
979 Third Avenue, 12th floor
New York, NY 10022
(212) 838-7878
brunschwig.com

Claremont
979 Third Avenue
New York, NY 10022
(212) 486-1252
Claremontfurnishing.com
Multiple locations

Clarence House
979 Third Avenue, Suite 205
New York, NY 10022
(212) 752-2890
clarencehouse.com
Multiple locations

Farrow and Ball
979 Third Avenue, Suite 1519
New York, NY 10022
(212) 752-5544
us.farrow-ball.com
Multiple locations

Holland and Sherry
979 Third Avenue
#1402
New York, NY 10022
(212) 355-6241
hollandandsherry.com
Multiple locations

Lee Jofa
979 Third Avenue, Suite 234
New York, NY 10022
(212) 688-0444
leejofa.com
Multiple locations

Meg Braff Designs
92 Forest Avenue
Locust Valley, NY 11560
(516) 801-4939
megbraffdesigns.com

Quadrille
quadrillefabrics.com

FRAMING

APF Master Framemakers
215 East 59th Street
New York, NY 10022
(212) 308-6152
apfmunn.com

Images & Details
19 Forest Avenue
Locust Valley, NY 11560
(516) 676-7320
imagesanddetailsframing.com

J. Pocker
135 East 63rd Street
New York, NY 10065
(212) 838-5488
Multiple locations

KITCHENS

Caesarstone
caesarstoneus.com

Fireclay Tile
fireclaytile.com

Mosaic House
32 West 22nd Street
New York, NY 10010
(212) 414-2525
mosaichse.com

Pirch
200 Lafayette Street
New York, NY 10012
(212) 951-0696
pirch.com
Multiple locations

Waterworks
215 East 58th Street
New York, NY 10022
(212) 371-9266
waterworks.com
Multiple locations

LIGHTING

Christopher Spitzmiller
christopherspitzmiller.com

Currey & Co.
curreyco.com

Franklin & Company
franklinandcompany.com

Genie House
geniehouse.com

vanCollier
vancollier.com

Vaughan Designs, Inc.
979 Third Avenue, Suite 1511
New York NY 10022
(212) 319-7070
vaughandesigns.com

Visual Comfort & Co.
visualcomfort.com

LINENS

Jane Wilner Designs
janewilnerdesigns.net

Leontine Linens
leontinelinens.com

Matouk
matouk.com

Satori Fine Linens
satorilinens.com

OUTDOOR

Brown Jordan
www.brownjordan.com

Janus et Cie
janusetcie.com

Lane Venture
laneventure.com

Munder Skiles
munder-skiles.com

Perennials
perennialsfabrics.com

Sunbrella
sunbrella.com

UPHOLSTERY

Billy Baldwin Studio
billybaldwinstudio.com

Century Furniture
centuryfurniture.com

Gonsman Drapery & Upholstery
(561) 732-8841

Hickory Chair
hickorychair.com

Lee Industries
leeindustries.com

Mrs. Howard
sherrillfurniture.com/
mrandmrshoward

Rosenfeld Interiors
rosenfeldinteriors.com

Acknowledgments

I WOULD LIKE TO START BY ACKNOWLEDGING MY WONDERFUL CLIENTS, WITHOUT WHOM NONE OF THIS WOULD HAVE BEEN POSSIBLE. Every day, I count my lucky stars to have been blessed with such devoted clients and friends. I have clients who started as friends and became clients, and clients who started as clients and became friends. I am ever so grateful for both.

To my amazing children, Douglas, Andrew, William, and Charles, who truly understand my passion for design and have been so supportive of my love of decorating. I hope that you each find something equally fulfilling someday.

To my charming husband, Doug, who, since we were married twenty-three years ago, has never known a day without my work tote bags cluttering his car or a strange piece of furniture taking up room in our garage. You are a gentleman and a dream of a husband in every way.

To the amazing Cali Ross, who has kept my office running smoothly with positive energy for years with her can-do approach to everything.

To my incredible staff, present and past, who have supported me in every way and without whom I could not have completed this body of work. It certainly takes a village and then some. Thank you for taking it all in stride.

To my friend and cherished design assistant, Amal Kapen, who helped me with many of these projects and was the stylist extraordinaire for all of the new photography in this book. It seems like an understatement to say I could not have done it without you. Thank you.

To my fellow Mississippian, Newell Turner, who first published my work and who has been a constant source of support and encouragement over the years.

To Josh Gibson, my very talented photographer, who has an amazing eye and a fabulous sense of humor.

To Brooke Showell, whose beautiful way with words helped me to write this book. You are a dream to work with.

Many thanks to my fabulous editor, Kathleen Jayes; to Charlotte Moss, who generously wrote my foreword and encouraged me to take on this project; to Doug Turshen and Steve Turner, who designed pages of beautiful text and photography and helped my work be its best; and to Jill Cohen, who helped me put together my amazing team. Thank you to all of you for guiding me through this process with friendly and professional support, optimism, and experienced eyes. I am so very grateful to you.

And finally, my greatest debt is to my two wonderful and adoring parents, Mary Elizabeth and Fayette Williams, who blessed me with a magical life growing up in Mississippi, raised me and my brother, Fayette, with kindness and decency, and inspired us to the best we could be. They are the two loveliest people that I know.

Photography Credits

All images including the front cover by J. Savage Gibson except:

Tria Giovan 42-47, 58, 60, 61, 104, 105, 110, 111 (bottom left), 112, 114, 118-120, 123, 124, 142, 143, 162, 163, 170, 175 (bottom left), 222, 228, back cover; Jessica Klewicki Glynn 182; Frances Janisch 106, 130; Thibault Jeanson 26, 70, 98; Photographs by Francesco Lagnese 6 (bottom left), 52, 54, 62, 88, 91, 136, 137, 174 (bottom right), 175 (top left), 186, 189, 190; Jeff McNamara 7 (bottom right), 92, 217; Nicholas Mele 2, 65, 108, 109; James Merrell c/o Ashley Klinger & Co. 20, 23, 36, 71, 102, 103, 138, 171; © Marco Ricca 34, 35, 96; RLJ Photography NYC 87; Photograph by Lisa Romerein 11 (top left); © Lisa Romerein/Getty Images 11 (center right, bottom right), 150; Annie Schlechter 6 (top left), 7 (top & bottom left), 8, 11 (top right, center & bottom left) 24, 55, 94, 164, 179, 180, 183, 195, 206; Simon Upton / The Interior Archive 56, 57, 64, 107, 157, 158, 190

First published in the United States of America in 2017
by Rizzoli International Publications, Inc.
300 Park Avenue South
New York, NY 10010
www.rizzoliusa.com

Copyright © 2017 Meg Braff

All rights reserved. No part of this publication may be reproduced, stored in a retrieval system, or transmitted in any form or by any means, electronic, mechanical, photocopying, recording, or otherwise, without prior consent of the publishers.

2017 2018 2019 2020 / 10 9 8 7 6 5 4 3 2 1

Distributed in the U.S. trade by Random House, New York

Designed by Doug Turshen with Steve Turner

Printed in China

ISBN-13: 978-0-8478-5872-9

Library of Congress Catalog Control Number: 2016953380